CHEAT CODE MARKETING

By Risyl Lejos

CONTENTS

TURNING FEELINGS INTO PROFIT

"The best marketing doesn't feel like marketing."

Tom Fishburne

T o write sales messages that really sell, you need to understand what makes us tick.

Fortunately, you don't need a PhD in psychology to convince people to hit that buy button, just a basic understanding of how our minds work.

Ultimately, the reasons we buy things seem logical and personal, but are actually driven by a range of predictable patterns that operate beneath our conscious awareness.

In this book, I'll take you inside the human mind and explain the subconscious mechanisms that shape our purchasing decisions.

Then I'll show you how to trigger and amplify these systems to make your offers irresistible.

This is key to transforming passive browsers into hungry customers desperate to buy from you again and again.

Once you've finished reading this book, you'll know everything you need to create a sales page that really sells.

I don't mean a handful of conversions a month to supplement your income from that full-time job you hate.

I mean you'll know how to create a sales page that rakes in thousands of dollars a month, every month, like clockwork.

It doesn't matter what niche you're in or what product or service you provide.

The principles you'll learn are as universal to humans as breathing.

Why a sales page?

If you can create a compelling sales page, you can repurpose and expand upon that content to build out your entire sales funnel.

A great sales page makes it a lot easier to write persuasive ad copy for emails, Facebook, Instagram, Twitter, Google, Amazon and more.

Better yet, the psychological principles and techniques underpinning a successful sales page have applications right across your entire business.

Once you understand them...

Once you practice them and make them automatic...

You'll be able to convert 100%, 200% up to 1,000% or more prospects, in less time and with far less effort!

WARNING

"As marketers, we should be changing the mantra from always be closing to always be helping."

Jonathan Lister

T he strategies and techniques you'll learn in this book are powerful, so please use them ethically.

The information is intended to help you frame your offers to customers in a more enticing and persuasive way.

Please don't use what you learn here to make promises you can't keep.

Return customers are the lifeblood of any successful online business.

But they'll only come back if they trust you.

And they'll only trust you if you deliver.

PART 1 – WHY

WHY DO WE BUY THINGS?

*"Our intuitions about what drives our be-
haviors are flawed."*

Dan Ariely

As consumers, we like to imagine our purchasing decisions are mostly rational.

That we buy things because we need them or they will help us achieve a practical goal – like vacuum the pet hair out of the car or whiten our coffee-stained teeth.

The truth is, we aren't always consciously aware of why we chose to buy things, especially why we favour one brand of product over another.

The psychological mechanisms influencing our decisions are largely subconscious.

Over the last few decades, advances in our understanding of human psychology and behaviour have revealed four fundamental truths you can harness in your marketing to dramatically boost your sales:

1. **Cognitive biases** influence our decisions.

2. **Emotions play** a major role in the choices we make.

3. **Dopamine**, the pleasure chemical, has a big impact on our behaviour.

4. **Choice** shapes our purchasing decisions in surprising ways.

In Part 1 of this book, we'll look at each of these influences in detail and explore how they can dramatically improve your marketing.

Then in Part 2, I'll show you how you can amplify their power to have your prospects begging to buy from you.

INFLUENCE 1 –
COGNITIVE BIASES

"Knowing that one may be subject to bias is one thing; being able to correct it is another."

Jon Eister

We buy things because we're biased.

We assume we only make decisions after thoroughly examining our options.

The truth is we're bombarded by so much information each day our brains tend to take shortcuts.

These shortcuts are called cognitive biases (or heuristics if you want to impress someone).

They're like mental reflexes in that they allow us to skip processing all our options and arrive straight at a decision.

They're surprisingly accurate most of the time, but they're also errors of thinking that shape our decisions in predictable ways.

How did these biases develop?

Imagine our prehistoric ancestors relaxing in a cave when they spot a shadow approaching.

They don't have time to wait for enough information to figure out whether it's a member of the tribe returning from a hunt or a sabretooth tiger browsing for lunch.

If they stop to think too long, they could be eaten.

So, they opt for the safest option and pick up their spears.

This subconscious reliance on strategies that have proven effective in the past still shapes a lot of our decisions today.

Although now, the same predictable patterns of thinking that help keep us safe can also be harnessed to influence our behaviour.

Our cognitive biases have been with us so long, they can be incredibly hard to resist, even when we're consciously aware of them.

They just feel right.

The power of the unconscious

Have you ever had to complete a task a certain way but had built a bad habit of doing it the wrong way?

And no matter how hard you tried you just couldn't do it right?

A few years ago, I took a copywriting gig that required me to switch from using a PC to a Mac.

I was using all the same word processing and design programs I was familiar with, but the layout of the Mac's interface kept tripping me up.

The buttons to open and close windows were in the left corner of the screen instead of the right.

I kept finding myself aimlessly clicking in the right corner while thinking about what I had to do next.

It was frustrating.

I was consciously aware I had to click in the left corner of the screen.

But clicking in the right corner was so ingrained, the second my mind wandered I would find myself doing it again.

That's how powerful these subconscious patterns can be.

What does this mean for your marketing?

Cognitive biases are like cheat codes for the human brain.

They provide a template of predictable decision-making patterns that you can exploit to supercharge your sales.

They allow you to influence your prospects' choices by framing your offers in a more persuasive way.

We're not talking brainwashing here, or making wildly exaggerated claims, just aligning your content with the way people's minds actually work to make your offers more appealing.

Cognitive bias triggers are everywhere

When you know what to look for, you'll see a lot of marketing already exploits cognitive biases in an unstructured way.

When you watch an ad on TV or drive past a billboard, you experience an advertiser attempting to trigger one or more cognitive biases in you.

These attempts are often clumsy and not as persuasive as they could be.

It's only when biases are triggered in a deliberate and coordinated way that they reveal their true influential power.

How many cognitive biases are there?

There are over 100 cognitive biases you can harness to boost your sales.

Don't worry, you don't have to remember 100 different strategies to become a better marketer.

Most cognitive biases are variations on a few key themes, and it's the most powerful of these themes that I've handpicked for you to use in your sales page.

The best biases for selling impact:
- attention
- memory, and
- decision-making.

They help you connect to your audience, deliver a message they'll remember and inspire them to take action.

We'll look at triggering cognitive biases in more detail in Part 2 of this book, but to get started, let's explore five cognitive biases that are great for attracting attention.

Bias 1: focusing effect

How it works

We tend to place too much importance on one aspect of an event – typically the part that most stands out.

How to use it

Make a bold, memorable statement that will resonate with your audience and be the first thing they recall about your product or service.

Bias 2: hot hand fallacy

How it works

We believe that someone who has experienced success has a greater chance of further success in additional attempts.

How to use it

Show undeniable proof of the success of your product or service so your prospect will assume this success will continue.

Bias 3: negativity bias

How it works

We recall negative memories more easily than positive ones.

How to use it

Ask negative questions that reaffirm your prospect's suspicions then raise their anticipation of a solution.

Bias 4: empathy gap

How it works

We tend to underestimate how powerful an influence our feelings are on our behaviour.

How to use it

Tell a warm, heartfelt story to connect with your prospect so they attach positive feelings to your product or service.

Bias 5: availability heuristic

How it works

Unusual or emotional memories are easier to recall and therefore have a larger influence on our behaviour.

How to use it

Lead with an unusual fact or feature of your product or service to spark interest and stand out from the crowd.

INFLUENCE 2 – EMOTIONS

*"We are not thinking machines. We are feel-
ing machines that think."*

Antonio Damasio

We buy things because we expect them to fulfil an emotional need.

The deeper the emotional connection, the more
likely we are to make a purchase.

The power of intuition

In his ground-breaking book *Thinking, Fast and Slow*, psychologist
Daniel Kahneman captures the outsized influence our emotions
have on our behaviour.

He breaks the way we think down into two distinct systems:
- System 1 – an automatic, fast and emotional way of
  thinking.
- System 2 – a deliberate, slow and rational way of thinking.

Research has revealed an astonishing 95% of our decisions are
driven by System 1, while only 5% are driven by System 2.

Feeling is choosing

About a decade ago, neuroscientist Antonio Damasio made an even more startling discovery.

While working with patients with damage to the part of the brain that generates emotions, he found they also couldn't make simple decisions, such as choosing what to eat.

The logical part of their brain still functioned normally, but without emotional feedback they couldn't make a choice.

They didn't know what they felt like eating, so an objective analysis of their options was virtually worthless.

Emotion beats analysis

Where a lot of online marketers go wrong is trying to win customers over using logic when our emotions are a much more powerful driver of our behaviour.

It might make logical sense for your prospect to buy your product, but if the purchase doesn't feel right to them, you'll lose the sale.

A great article by renowned psychologist Dan Ariely '3 main lessons of psychology', captures just how profoundly our emotions shape our choices.

Dan explains that people will donate more money to starving children in Africa if they hear the story of a single child rather than two children.

It's easier for us to empathise with the needs of one child because the needs of two or more children become emotionally overwhelming as their situation seems hopeless.

Our emotions connect us deeply to each other's pain and yet numb us when that pain becomes too large.

Although we rarely have to deal with such emotionally challenging issues in online marketing, the underlying principles driving human connection still apply.

If you want to sell more effectively, you have to connect your solution to your prospect's deep emotional needs.

To do that, you need to learn more about your ideal customer.

Who is your ideal customer?

Your ideal customer is someone starving for your product or service.

They're not an aimless browser who stumbles upon your page and finds it interesting – though we'll convert them too.

Your ideal customer is a person with a deep emotional need for the solution your product or service provides.

They're ideal because you can provide them with the most value, and they're likely to provide you with the most value in return – through repeat purchases, positive reviews, testimonials and raving about your product or service to their friends and family.

Targeting your content at their needs enables you to create the most authentic, inspiring and compelling sales journey.

Why?

Because your solution is perfect for them.

What do they need?

Grab a pen and paper or jot some notes down on your smartphone or computer.

Keep your notes somewhere safe as they will form a basic profile of your ideal customer that you'll refer back to when you write your copy.

Imagine your ideal customer sitting across from you and answer the following questions.

To help you get started, I've written example answers for a fictional diet product I've called Carb Cycle.

What is the problem your ideal customer is dying for you to solve?

My ideal customer is desperate to lose weight without having to survive on bland, boring diet foods.

How does this problem make them feel?

They feel frustrated, helpless and hopeless. They feel like they've been scammed by other diet providers and ashamed of their body.

How does your product or service solve their problem?

Carb Cycle is a healthy eating plan that helps you rapidly lose weight while still enjoying the foods you love.

How would your ideal customer feel about solving their problem?

They'd feel proud to have achieved their goal weight, more confident at work, the beach and going out.

They'd have more energy to play with their kids, and feel more attractive to their partner or their date.

Sharpen your profile

Now that you have a profile of your ideal customer, it's time to see how well it aligns with reality and fill in any gaps.

Do some research online for similar products or services in your niche and look at reviews and comments.

Amazon is a great tool for this due to the enormous range of products it offers and the number of customer reviews it attracts.

Google, eBay and specialist online stores in your niche are great options too.

Make a list of the most common questions, comments or complaints customers have and score them by how frequently they appear.

Now go back to your profile and see if you captured the three most common. Also, check to see if the language you've used aligns with how prospective customers describe their problems.

Don't get carried away

Like a lot of things in marketing, it's better to be good and on time than perfect and late when it comes to profiling your ideal customer.

Beyond a certain point, research can become counterproductive, especially if it dampens your enthusiasm for selling your product.

The truth is the profile you build doesn't have to be perfect at first.

You just need a rough guide to target your content.

Once you publish your page and have some live data, you can hone your profile further.

Emotions to trigger

There are hundreds of emotions you can stimulate to boost your sales.

Seven of these are vital for creating a supercharged sales strategy.

Anticipation – motivates us to keep moving forward.

Surprise – shakes us out of complacency and inspires us to seek answers.

Anger – drives us to find new solutions to old frustrations.

Hope – inspires us to look optimistically to the future.

Trust – soothes our fears and gives us faith.

Excitement – makes us come alive, encourages us to act and take a chance.

Fear – of losing something valuable can spur us into action.

Getting the balance right

The best marketing triggers emotions like a classic adventure movie.

It takes you from challenging lows to exciting highs as it builds to a rousing resolution.

An influential message strikes a balance of emotions that leans toward optimism.

Too negative and your message will be depressing and demotivating.

Too positive and it will ring false.

The right tone is both positive and realistic.

You're not denying the scope of the problem, but you're confident in your solution and the benefits it delivers.

INFLUENCE 3 – DOPAMINE

"...dopamine...is about the happiness of pursuit of reward that has a decent chance of occurring."

Robert M. Sapolsky

We buy things because they make us feel good. Our brains release the pleasure chemical dopamine when we even consider making a purchase.

It's the drug of anticipation that surges when we expect a reward.

It drives us to explore the world and make new discoveries that will increase our chances of survival.

Driven to anticipate

The neuroscientist Robert M. Sapolsky devised an ingenious experiment to study the effect dopamine has on the brain.

He trained monkeys to wait for a light to switch on and then press a button ten times to receive a treat.

He discovered the monkeys received a surge of dopamine when the light came on that subsided while they were pressing the button.

Neurochemically, they received the reward before they received the reward.

Interestingly, he found that if he added uncertainty, only delivering the treat half the time, twice as much dopamine was released in the monkey's brain when the light came on.

By adding uncertainty, he had effectively doubled the monkey's anticipation for the reward.

This combination of anticipation and uncertainty of reward is incredibly powerful and can be incorporated into your sales page to make your offers much more appealing.

Who does it well?

You can see the impact dopamine has on our behaviour in gaming.

The potential reward of completing a stage or killing an enemy, added to the uncertainty of achieving that goal, and a whole host of visual and audio cues designed to ramp up anticipation, can make games incredibly addictive.

Mobile games are particularly good at leveraging anticipation and uncertainty of reward to encourage users to trial and then purchase products in an incredibly competitive marketplace.

How to trigger dopamine

The simplest way to harness the influence of dopamine in your sales page is to follow three key principles.

1. Frame your offer as a reward – write your content like you're delivering real satisfaction for your customer, not just a superficial solution to their problem.

Use active, personal language that positions your product or service as a fulfilling reward at the end of a long road of frustration and disappointment.

2. Build anticipation of the delivery of the reward – use a diverse mix of enticing headlines, personal stories, unusual information, checklists, customer testimonials, product details, sales buttons and media to build a nuanced, exciting picture of your offer.

3. Introduce uncertainty about the delivery of the reward – use limited time offers, bonus deals, introductory prices, reduced rate bundles and other temporary offers to spike dopamine at the purchase stage.

Is this ethical?

Strategies designed to trigger dopamine have come in for criticism recently due to their use in online gambling.

Online gambling providers engineer their apps and platforms to hook users in a cycle of never ending uncertainty.

But whereas they aim to keep their customers online, handing over money for the slim chance to win, you'll be marketing a product or service that will add real value to your customers' lives, and they can access the benefits right away.

If you ask me, that's a win-win situation for everyone.

It's important to remember too that dopamine is triggered naturally in the brain and all you're really doing is presenting your offer in a way that invites anticipation.

Your goal isn't to create dopamine addicts or take advantage of anyone, it's to empathise with your prospect's problems and lead them on an exciting journey to their solution.

INFLUENCE 4 – CHOICE

"Make your product easier to buy than your competition, or you will find customers buying from them, not you."

Mark Cuban

We buy things when we think we're making the right choice.

The fewer options we have, the easier it is for us to choose one and be happy with it.

Don't let choice ruin your sale

Introduce too many options too early in your sales page and you risk creating analysis paralysis – where there are so many choices available to your prospect they become overwhelmed and give up.

You want your prospect to know the only reason you are promoting a specific solution to their problem is because it's the best solution for the job.

If you introduce too many options, you're asking the prospect to choose the solution that's best for them – but you should know the solution that's best for them and be able to explain why.

The science behind the theory

In 2000, Sheena Lyengar and Mark Lepper of Columbia and Stanford Universities found an ingeniously simple way to test how choice affects our purchasing behaviour.

They set up a stall offering jam samples outside a store in Menlo Park, California.

On two consecutive Saturdays, they offered shoppers a selection of 24 and then 6 flavours of jam to sample.

The results were fascinating, if counter intuitive.

On the day they offered 24 flavours, 60% of people stopped to sample Jams.

On the day they offered 6 flavours, only 40% of people stopped to try a sample.

That makes sense, right? Offer more choice, get more customers.

The surprise came when they looked at purchases.

Of the customers who sampled 24 flavours, only 3% bought jam.

Of the customers who sampled 6, 30% made a purchase.

If 100 people had passed by the stall on both days, that's 2 sales vs 12.

By offering less choice, Sheena and Mark were able to significantly increase their chances of making a sale.

Solve one problem completely

When creating a sales page, focus on completely solving one problem for your prospect and offering them a chance to make a purchase before moving on to additional offers.

Some problems are multifaceted, so you may need to write about a range of subjects to solve them.

That's fine, so long as every word you write, image you select, video you include is designed to solve one overarching problem and drive the purchase of just one or as few products as possible.

If you run an eCommerce store with lots of products laid out in a catalogue-style display, look for opportunities to group them into larger themes and then create individual sales pages for each theme.

For example, if you run a fashion store, you could group outfits for the party season.

This allows you to simplify your offers to prospects while also providing them the flexibility to explore your catalogue.

If you want to provide upsell and cross-sell opportunities, make sure you only offer them after you have completely solved a problem and given the prospect the chance to make a purchase.

You can do this by either offering upsell/cross-sell opportunities beneath the purchase button for a product or on the purchase confirmation screen.

Why?

One of the key reasons you want to limit choice is to amplify the effect of a powerful cognitive bias...

The sunk cost fallacy

How it works

The more energy, time or money we invest in something, the more likely we are to continue investing, even if we don't achieve the result we want.

Cutting our losses feels like admitting defeat, even if it is the most rational course of action.

Have you ever purchased too much food for an event and felt obligated to eat more than you really wanted to avoid having to throw it away?

That's the sunk cost fallacy at work.

How to use it

By limiting each sales page to solving one problem and providing one product, you invite the prospect to invest a significant amount of time and energy in learning more about your solution.

This investment is effectively wasted if they fail to make a purchase.

Similarly, just before or after a purchase is made, upsell or cross-sell offers are much more persuasive as the customer has already committed to investing money in your product or service and may as well invest a little more to unlock its full potential.

This is why online clothing stores will prompt you to 'complete the outfit' with accessories when you review your shopping cart.

You're already going to buy the jeans, why not grab the socks too?

AMPLIFYING THE BIG 4

Separately, our cognitive biases, emotions, dopamine and choices are powerful drivers of our behaviour.

Combined, they're superpowered sales weapons.

The best way to amplify their influence is through a **Cognitively Optimised Sales Structure (COSS)** that employs:

1. Bias stacking

To unlock the full potential of cognitive biases, you need to stack them on top of each other, exploiting multiple mental shortcuts as you gradually amplify the influence of your message.

2. Structured emotional journey

Armed with a profile of your ideal customer, use active, empathetic language to connect with their deep emotional needs and guide them through a structured sequence of feelings that resolve with a purchase.

3. Strategic dopamine triggers

Build anticipation throughout the sales journey by triggering dopamine at specific intervals, culminating in the highest spikes at the purchase stage.

4. Limiting choice

Limit each **COSS** to the promotion of a single theme, product or service.

If you have multiple themes/products/services to promote, create multiple strategies and link them to together.

How long should the COSS be?

Your sales page should be around 2,000 words in total as this will help your page rank higher in Google and convert more browsers.

This word count will also help you establish your authority in the niche and provide enough detail to convince your prospect to make a purchase.

What does it look like?

A **COSS** has five phases built up over five stages.

It's designed to efficiently move a prospect from discovering your page to making an excited purchase.

It grabs the prospect's attention and gradually encourages them to invest more time in learning about your solution by providing increasing amounts of detail.

This layering of detail helps to amplify the effect of the sunk cost fallacy while also increasing a prospect's time on site and exposure to other techniques of persuasion.

Over the next five pages, we'll build a **COSS** from scratch so you can see how the individual components fit together.

Then in Part 2, I'll take you through how to create content for each phase with examples from profitable niche markets.

STAGE 1

The **COSS** leads a prospect through five phases each with specific content, emotional and chemical objectives.

STAGE 2

Anticipation builds throughout all five phases, reaching its peak in the **Convert Phase**.

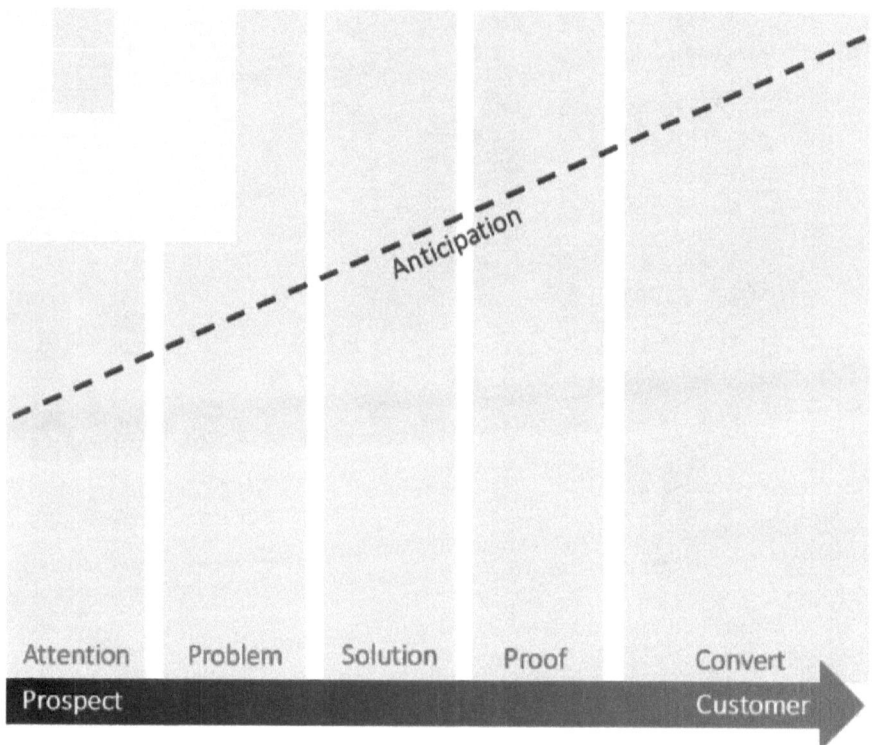

STAGE 3

Dopamine is triggered at strategic intervals to build momentum until the prospect is primed to purchase.

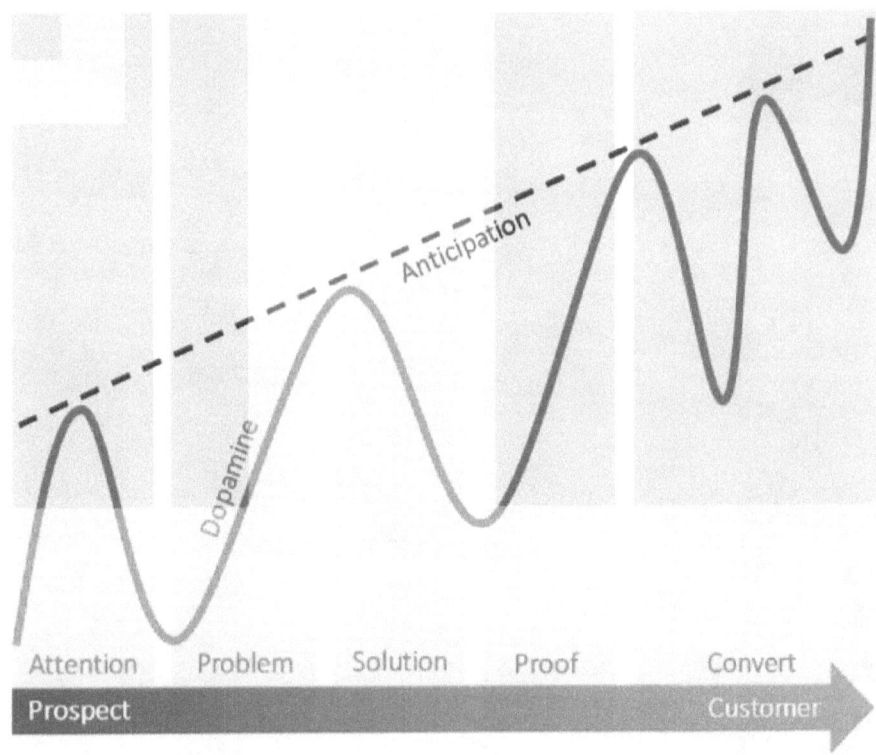

STAGE 4

Specific emotions are triggered during each phase to connect the product or service to a prospect's deep emotional needs.

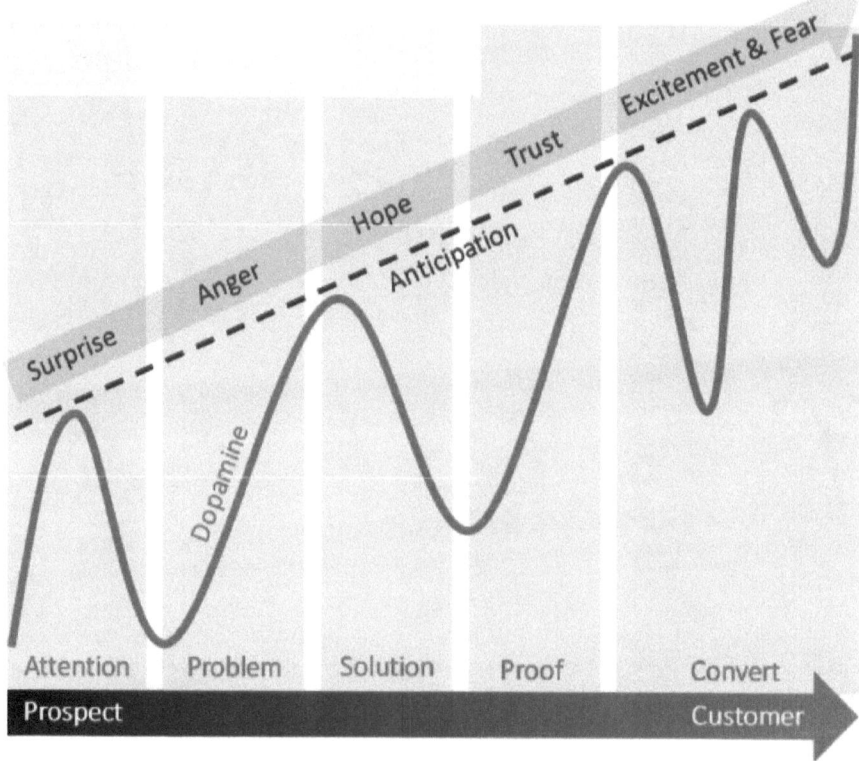

STAGE 5

Three limited offers are made during the **Convert Phase** to maximise uncertainty, spike dopamine and drive a purchase.

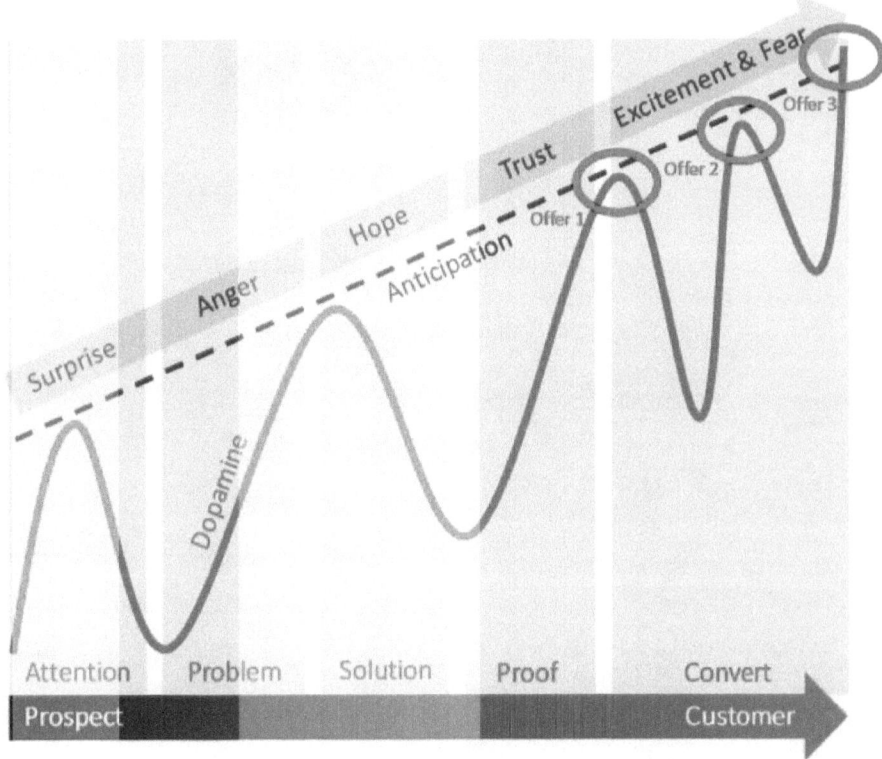

PART 2 – HOW

PHASE 1 – ATTENTION

T he Attention Phase is the most important phase of your sales page.

It incorporates your lead video or image, headline and sub-headline.

If you fail to capture a prospect's interest here, the rest of your efforts will be wasted.

To succeed, you need to cut through the noise with a strong and distinctive message.

Content objective

Provide just enough information about your product or service and the problem it solves to entice the prospect to find out more.

Emotional objective

Surprise your prospect with an unexpectedly powerful and magnetic message.

Chemical objective

Induce a spike in dopamine to heighten anticipation.

How to layout your page

Lead with a large widescreen video or image at the top of the page to immediately grab your prospect's interest.

This will allow you to take advantage of the **picture superiority effect** which shows we recall pictures more easily than words.

We also tend to learn concepts more easily when they are expressed in images.

Scripting your video

Once you finish writing your page copy, you can use it as a script for a video.

That way it doesn't matter if your prospect watches the video or reads your page, they experience the same journey.

Video is extremely popular on social media, so don't forget to add captions so you can promote your video through your social channels.

85% of video on Facebook is watched without sound and 52% of all website traffic comes from mobile phones.

So, there's a good chance the prospect will want to see what you're offering without disturbing the person next to them.

Selecting your image

The right image can make a good page great and a great page sensational.

Look for an image that stands out, is well lit and clearly communicates a single concept.

Stock photos

Stock shots get a bad rap for being overly posed and fake, but they can work well if you take the time to find interesting natural shots that suit your niche.

Sites with good royalty free pics include:
- **pexels.com**

- **pixabay.com**
- **unsplash.com**
- **freeimages.com**

Professional photos

If you have the budget, professional shots are a great choice.

Whether you invest in the equipment to take them yourself or commission a photographer, unique professional shots can become an iconic signifier for your brand.

The important thing is to pick a style and stick with it to ensure your page is cohesive.

Headline

The headline you create will make or break your page.

Website data shows 80% of people read headlines, but only 20% go on to read the rest of the page.

To write headlines that sell, follow three key principles:

1. Evoke strong emotions

Think about the biggest problem your ideal customer faces and then imagine what it would mean to them to have it solved.

Proudly show off your amazing bikini body this summer with our 12-week Beach Ready Boot Camp!

...is better than...

Get fit for summer in just 12 weeks!

2. Be specific

A lot of marketers think a generic headline will appeal to a general audience, but all you really achieve with a broad headline is being dull and forgettable.

Numbers and specific pieces of information help to make your offers more targeted, credible and persuasive.

I made an amazing $3,648 in just 30 minutes following foolproof trading tips from veteran NYSE traders!

...is better than...

Boost your income with our trading tips!

3. Use as few words as possible

Notice I didn't say 'keep it short'.

The length of your headline typically depends on the complexity of the information you need to convey.

The goal is to deliver the most magnetic message in as few words as possible.

Subheadline

Traditionally, the subheadline provided more detail about your product or service as your headline focused on its benefits.

But now, we're all bombarded with so much content each day, you need to convey as much detail as possible in your headline to grab people's attention.

Your subheadline then is an opportunity to reinforce your offer or highlight a unique and memorable fact or feature.

For example, if your headline was:

Bank $2,000 a month from this insanely simple 30-minute website build!

Your subheadline could be something like:

You'll be kicking yourself you don't have one of these already

...or...

It's so easy to create, just drag and drop

What does it look like?

To bring the different elements of the **Attention Phase** together in a cohesive way, you need a strategy.

The five cognitive biases we looked at on page 8 provide some excellent options.

Strategy 1 – Make a bold claim

Take advantage of the focusing effect and make a short, bold statement your audience will remember.

Example niche: weight loss

Headline

Lose 2 kilos a week eating pizza and watching Netflix!

Sub-headline

Okay, so you won't only be eating pizza, but it's still on the menu...

Strategy 2 – Show undeniable proof

Harness the hot hand fallacy and show impressive evidence of the success of your solution to lend credibility to your offer.

Example niche: making money online

Share a photo of a cheque or account balance that proves you have made a tonne of money with your product.

Headline

Working just 5 hours a week, I made $10,423 in a month from affiliate marketing!

Subheadline

If you can use a computer, you can do it too

Strategy 3 – Ask intriguing questions

Trigger your prospect's negativity bias by asking questions that reaffirm their suspicions, then raise their anticipation of a solution.

Example niche: dating

Stacked headline and subheadline

Tired of dates that go nowhere?

Sick of putting yourself out there only to be disappointed time and time again?

Want a foolproof way to attract the women you really like?

Strategy 4 – Tell an emotional story

Take advantage of your prospect's empathy gap and tell a story designed to engage their emotions rather than provide technical details about the product or service.

This strategy works particularly well for the self-improvement and wellness niches where the goals aren't as tangible.

Example niche: self help

Headline

Your pulse thuds in your ears. Your hands tremble. Your mouth is dry. You look out at a blur of faces and can't remember a thing...

Subheadline

You take a deep breath, run through the Perfect Calm routine and deliver your presentation with confidence.

Strategy 5 – Highlight a strange fact or feature

Trigger the availability heuristic and make your offer more memorable by highlighting an unusual fact or feature of your product or service.

Example niche: pets

Headline

Playing hide-and-seek as a kid taught me everything I needed to toilet train my pug!

Subheadline

You won't believe how easy and fun this is

Advertising your page

With the content you've created for the Attention Phase fresh in your mind, it's time to create a few variations of teaser headline that you can promote through social media, ads and emails.

Whereas your sales page headline and subheadline are designed to encourage your prospect to read on, your ads need to be interesting enough that your prospect just can't help but click through to find out more.

Fortunately, there's another powerful cognitive bias you can harness to dramatically boost interest in your offer.

Curiosity tendency bias

How it works

Humans are the most curious animals on Earth.

Our curiosity helps us develop a deeper understanding of ourselves and the world around us, increasing our odds of survival.

How to use it

Create a curiosity gap in your headline that can only be resolved if the prospect clicks through to your sales page to find out more.

This type of headline creates a broken loop that we curious mammals find incredibly hard to resist trying to resolve.

Who does it well?

News and entertainment sites such as Buzzfeed and Upworthy are masters of the curiosity gap.

They publish thousands of content pieces each day in an extremely competitive environment.

They rely on headlines that harness the curiosity gap for one simple reason: they work, bringing in tens of millions of pageviews each month.

Creating curiosity

To create a curiosity gap:
1. Share a piece of information.
2. Leave a piece of information out that your prospect will be desperate to know.

You can do this by either splitting the headline in two or focusing on the missing information in a single line.

Example niche: fitness

Headline 1 – two lines

Shredded guys swear by this ab exercise. Is it part of your routine?

Headline 2 – one line

14 insane exercise tweaks that separate the jacked from the weekend warrior

PHASE 2 – PROBLEM

N ow that you have your prospect's attention, the **Problem Phase** is your chance to connect with their deep emotional needs.

It's a vital stage as it allows you to establish empathy by showing you understand your prospect's frustration, and then aggravate it to motivate them to find a solution.

Content objective

Frame the problem in a way that's familiar to your prospect, then show them it's larger and more complex than they imagine – this helps justify why they've been unsuccessful in solving the problem so far.

Emotional objective

Amplify the prospect's frustration with solving the problem to generate anger as motivation.

Chemical objective

Dopamine subsides and is replaced with the stress hormone cortisol, amplifying the brain's desire for another reward.

Cognitive biases to target

The strategy in this phase is informed by two powerful cognitive biases that impact the prospect's perception and beliefs about the problem they face.

Confirmation bias

How it works

We tend to focus on and remember information that confirms our preconceptions about the world.

How to use it

Start the Problem Phase by confirming your prospect's preconceptions about the problem they face.

Pessimism bias

How it works

We tend to overestimate the chance of negative events happening to us.

How to use it

Harness the prospect's fears about the problem and exacerbate them with information of which they probably aren't aware.

Planning the copy

Now that you know what you want to achieve, how do you do it?

First, split the problem into what the prospect knows and what they don't know.

Next, write around 200 words for each, for a total of about 400 words for the phase.

To generate ideas for what to include in the paragraphs, go back to your profile of your ideal customer and then expand on your original answers by addressing the questions on the following page.

I've included example answers for the fictional product Carb Cycle again for reference.

What they know

What is the problem?

My ideal customer struggles to lose weight.

They find dieting difficult and boring.

If they do lose weight, they always end up gaining it back plus a few extra pounds/kilos.

How does the problem make your ideal customer feel?

They feel frustrated, helpless and hopeless.

They feel like they've spent most of their life trying to get their weight under control.

They feel like they've been scammed by diet gurus and cynical about the diet industry.

They feel ashamed of their body and disappointed in themselves for not sorting their weight problem out sooner.

How have others tried and failed to solve the problem in the past?

Low calorie diets just starve you until your willpower fails and you stuff your face.

Intermittent fasting is impractical as it only allows you to eat within a small window. It also leads to binge-eating as you are so hungry by the time you get a meal, you convince yourself you've earned a treat.

Diet shakes are bland, powdery and boring. It's the same thing day in, day out and leads you to crave junk food.

Ultra-healthy diets are unrealistic as they ask you to give up too many of the foods you enjoy.

No-carb diets just leave you tired and mess with your body's natural processing of sugar.

What they don't know

What are three statistics your prospect may not know about the problem?

1. *According to the World Health Organisation, worldwide obesity has nearly tripled since 1975.*
2. *39% of adults aged 18 years and over were overweight in 2016, and 13% were obese.*
3. *41 million children under the age of 5 were overweight or obese in 2016.*

What are three facts your prospect may not know about the problem?

1. *Leptin is a chemical produced by your body's fat cells. The more body fat you have, the more leptin your body produces.*
2. *Leptin tells the hypothalamus in your brain how much body fat you have as it controls when and how much you eat, and how fast your metabolism burns.*
3. *Most obese people are leptin resistant – they have a lot of leptin in their blood but it doesn't register in their hypothalamus so they overeat and store fat easily.*

Writing the copy

To write the copy, simply choose a perspective and tie your answers to the questions together in a seamless narrative.

On the following page, I've opted for the first person perspective (I, we) as it will help me display more empathy.

The second person perspective (you) is just as effective for less personal offers, and is superior for listing features and conversion copy.

[What they know – 200 words]

I grabbed a handful of flab around my waist and sobbed.

It's embarrassing to admit, but it's true.

I was getting dressed for work and it all just hit me at once:

- *How disappointed I was in myself for letting my weight get so bad.*
- *How tired I was of dieting and failing and trying again, over and over.*
- *How frustrated I was with occasionally losing a kilo or two only to watch the weight come back and more when my will-power eventually broke.*

I sat depressed on the end of my bed and thought about all the diets I'd tried.

The endless hours I'd spent starving myself, waiting for the evening to come around so I binge on pizza, chips and chocolate.

The days spent sucking down bland, powdery diet shakes with their phony flavours.

The months I'd tried to stick to a no-carbohydrate diet only to lose energy and become so hyper-reactive to sugar, a night of casual drinking would give me panic attacks.

That's when the heavy feeling of sadness in my chest turned hot with anger.

I was sick of being taken by money-hungry diet gurus flogging the next worthless fad.

I made a promise to myself right then and there that I would sort this shit out once and for all.

[What they don't know – 200 words]

I dedicated the next year of my life to learning everything I could about nutrition and weight loss.

I booked a consultation with a nutritionist named Sam and picked his brain on why losing weight was so hard for me.

That's when I discovered the problem was so much bigger than the few extra kilos around my waist:

- *According to the World Health Organisation, worldwide obesity has nearly tripled since 1975.*
- *39% of adults aged 18 years and over are overweight, and 13% are obese.*
- *Worse, 41 million children under 5 are overweight or obese.*

I asked Sam why was this happening?

Why was the whole world getting fatter each year?

His answer: leptin resistance.

Leptin is a hormone produced by our fat cells that helps our bodies regulate our weight.

It tells the part of our brain that controls our hunger, the hypothalamus, to stop sending hunger signals when we've had enough to eat.

The hypothalamus also controls our metabolism which regulates how fast we burn energy.

Most obese people have very high levels of leptin in their blood that doesn't register in their brains, so they overeat and their metabolism slows.

PHASE 3 – SOLUTION

Y our prospect knows you understand their pain.
Now, it's time to solve it.

The **Solution Phase** is your chance to:
- showcase your product or service
- explain how and why it works in detail, and
- show why it's superior to the competition.

If a prospect has reached this phase, it's safe to assume they are interested in learning more about your offer.

Provide the information they need in the format they need it and you're one step closer to making a sale.

Content objective

Show the prospect how your product or service solves their problem in detail, then help them imagine a future where their problem is solved.

Emotional objective

Harness the satisfaction provided by the solution to fill the prospect with hope for a better future.

Chemical objective

Trigger another spike of dopamine to increase anticipation.

The deal is in the detail

Providing prospects with detailed and accurate information about your solution is vital for making a sale.

A 2016 study from Label Insight found 73% of consumers consider transparency more important than price.

Surprisingly, nearly 40% said they would switch from their preferred brand to one that offered more transparency.

It may seem laborious to write, but providing detailed information about your solution will help you get more sales.

Cognitive biases to target

There are three cognitive biases to target in this phase that affect the way we engage with and process new information.

Information bias

How it works

As evidenced in the research above, this bias shows we generally prefer lots of information to support us when making decisions, even if some of it is unnecessary.

How to use it

When describing your product or service, include lots of intricate detail to provide a complete picture of your solution.

Your prospect might skim over it, but the extra information will help to reassure them that the solution is credible, ethically produced and well-considered.

Belief bias

How it works

We tend to consider an argument logical if we believe in the conclusion it proposes.

How to use it

Convince the prospect to believe in your solution by showing them how it will help them personally and what it will feel like to have their problem solved.

Backfire effect

How it works

We often react to information that contradicts our beliefs by strengthening them. If you've ever questioned someone's political or religious beliefs, you'll know the power of this bias.

How to use it

Don't tell people their beliefs about their problems are wrong, show them.

Ask them to imagine a future where your product or service has solved their problem.

Get them to feel the sense of satisfaction and relief as these emotions are far more persuasive than any logical argument.

Planning the copy

Break the content up into three sections of around 200 words each and cover:
- Detailed information about the solution – explaining the features and how it works.
- Personal information about the solution – listing the benefits to the prospect.
- A future state projection – to help the prospect imagine what it will feel like to have their problem solved.

Detailed information

What are five important features of your solution?

1. *Reverses leptin resistance – and helps your body reset your metabolism.*
2. *6 to 1 diet – eat a reduced carbohydrate diet for 6 days and you can eat whatever you like on day 7.*
3. *Flexible 8-hour eating window – eat your first meal then ensure your last meal is consumed within the 8-hour window.*
4. *Shopping guide – explaining foods to eat, foods to avoid and foods to save for cheat day.*
5. *Recipe guide – over 100 healthy meals you can make in just minutes each day.*

Personal information

How will these features benefit your ideal customer?

1. *You feel fuller for longer after meals and burn more calories even while you're watching TV.*
2. *One designated cheat day each week means you still get to treat yourself to all your favourite foods.*
3. *Eating only during an 8-hour window allows you to take advantage of the fat fighting benefits of intermittent fasting without starving or sacrificing your social life.*
4. *Knowing what to buy at the supermarket makes it easy and fun to stick to your plan.*
5. *Having a whole book of recipes ready to go makes preparing health, nutritious meals easy.*

Future state projection

What are five benefits of solving the problem your ideal customer could experience in the future?

They'll feel more:

1. *Comfortable showing off their body at the beach.*
2. *Confident in how they look at work and when they're out with friends.*
3. *Energy to play with their kids and enjoy a more active lifestyle.*
4. *Attractive to their partner or their date.*

5. *Pride and satisfaction in themselves and what they're able to achieve.*

Writing the copy

Pick up the narrative from where you left off in the Problem Phase and use bold text and bullet points to highlight the product features and benefits to assist the prospect in evaluating the offer.

When describing the features and benefits of the solution, switch to the second person perspective (you) as this will assist the prospect in visualising how the solution will benefit them.

Some people will tell you not to switch perspectives like this, but it can be an effective way to mimic how people really think and communicate.

It's also important to remember, you're not trying to win a grammar prize with your sales copy, you're just trying to convince the prospect to hit the buy button.

[Detailed information – 200 words]

Reversing leptin resistance isn't easy, but it's a surefire way to lose weight and keep it off.

For the next few months, fighting leptin resistance became my singular obsession.

I read everything Sam gave me on the subject, filled notebooks with diet ideas and worked with Sam to create an ultra-effective and realistic plan to lose massive amounts of weight and keep it off.

The result is Carb Cycle – a healthy eating program designed to reset your body's natural responses to food by:

- ***Reversing leptin resistance** – lowering the amount of leptin in your blood and increasing your brain's sensitivity to it.*
- ***Cycling low and high carbohydrate meals** – eat low carb for 6 days each week and you can eat whatever you like on day 7.*
- ***Limiting eating during an 8-hour window** – eat your first*

meal and make sure your last meal is consumed within 8 hours.

- **Cutting down on processed foods** – *by following a detailed shopping guide explaining foods to eat, foods to avoid and foods to save for cheat day.*
- **Preparing tasty, nutritious meals at home** – *from a recipe guide with over 100 meals you can make in just minutes each day.*

The big question: does it really work?

After a week of following Carb Cycle, I shook off sugar withdrawal, started feeling really good and had already lost a kilo.

[Personal information – 200 words]

After 1 month, I'd lost 6 kilos and had more energy.

After 3 months, I'd lost 15 kilos, dropped 2 sizes in jeans and felt better than I had in years.

Not only had I lost weight, but my mood had improved. I felt less anxious and more confident.

I've now been on the program for over a year, lost 32 kilos and kept it off!

There are so many benefits to eating this way:

Feel fuller for longer – as your brain's sensitivity to leptin improves, you won't spend all day ignoring hunger pains.

Still enjoy your favourite meals – one day each week you can binge on pizza, pasta, burgers and ice cream while still losing weight!

All the benefits of intermittent fasting without the starvation – Have your first meal when you want and finish with dinner 8 hours later. Too easy.

The shopping guide makes it easy to get what you need from the supermarket – Knowing what to buy means you're less likely to stock up on junk. And if there's no junk in the pantry, you're not going to eat it.

The recipe guide makes it a breeze to create simple, tasty meals at home – these healthy and delicious meals are so easy to make, anyone can do it.

[Future state projection – 200 words]

Carb Cycle didn't just help me lose weight, it completely changed my life.

This program did so much more for me than shift a few kilos.

Imagine heading to the beach without worrying about how you look in your swimwear because you know you look amazing.

Imagine feeling more confident at work and out with friends because you feel and look like you've always wanted.

Imagine having oodles of energy to chase around your kids, hike, bike, run and explore because you're finally giving your body the healthy natural fuel it needs.

Imagine feeling more sexy to your partner or heading out on a date knowing your body reflects the person you feel inside.

Imagine the feeling of pride and satisfaction when you look into the mirror and see the person you want to be staring back at you.

That's what I've experienced on this program.

Making the decision to follow Carb Cycle is the single best thing I have ever done for my health and wellbeing.

I have never felt this energised, happy and satisfied with myself.

If you follow this program, I know you'll feel it too.

PHASE 4 – PROOF

You've revealed your solution and shown the prospect how it can improve their life.

Now, you need to convince them you can deliver.

The **Proof Phase** is your chance to:
- prove your solution works, and
- earn your prospect's trust.

Content objective

Establish your authority in the niche and prove your solution works with evidence from a broad range of people, perspectives and applications.

Emotional objective

Earn the prospect's trust in you as a provider and in your solution to their problem.

Chemical objective

The bonding chemical Oxytocin replaces dopamine as you convince the prospect it's safe to put their faith in you. This primes the brain for the rapid fire reward seeking in the convert phase.

The importance of trust

We've all bought something before that didn't live up to the promises set in its marketing.

It's horrible to feel you've been duped and damages your trust in the product, the brand that produced it and the store that provided it, sometimes irreparably.

It's no surprise then that a study by Bizrate Insights found over 80% of online shoppers look for ratings and reviews while sizing up a new purchase.

And around 40% of online shoppers will only buy something if ratings and reviews are available.

Prospects want to know they can trust you, that's why it's vital you share success stories and testimonials from satisfied customers to back up the claims in your marketing.

Cognitive biases to target

There are two key biases to target during this phase to focus on how our brains rate and categorise new information.

Conjunction fallacy

How it works

We tend to assume specific information is more credible than general information.

How to use it

Ask for feedback and testimonials from customers that focus on specific rather than general benefits of your product or service.

Feedback that really drills into a specific and unique benefit is much more influential than a general "It works and I like it".

Cheerleader effect

How it works

We tend to find people more attractive in a group than alone. This is due to our brains taking a general snapshot of the faces and averaging out the less attractive features.

How to use it

Gather testimonials from a range of different people to show the breadth of benefits your product or service provides.

Earning the prospect's trust

Earning trust takes time and incorporates many factors that are beyond the scope of your sales page like:

- how individual customers experience your solution, and
- how you respond to feedback and complaints.

You can however display trustworthiness in your sales page, and begin the process of building a lasting relationship with your customer.

The quickest and easiest way to do this is to ensure your page demonstrates the '4 Cores of Credibility' established by Stephen M. R. Covey in his brilliant book *The Speed of Trust*.

Covey explains that trust is made up of two pairs of attributes that show character and competence.

CHARACTER

Integrity – Do your actions match your words?

What it means

Does your solution do what you say it will? Do you keep your promises and deliver?

How to show it

The quality of your product or service and your interactions with customers are the best ways to demonstrate your integrity.

The next best way is through customer testimonials, ratings and feedback.

Intent – What's your goal?

What it means

Why are you offering your product or service?

How to show it

Explain what motivated you to create your solution so the prospect understands why you want to help them.

COMPETENCE

Capabilities – Are you skilled?

What it means

How did you develop your product or service? What qualifications or skills do you have in the field?

How to show it

If you're an expert, explain your background and experience to legitimise your solution.

If you're a novice, explain the process that led you to develop your solution and highlight the expertise of anyone you consulted.

Results – Do you deliver?

What it means

What have you achieved in the past? What are you achieving now? How will you perform in the future?

How to show it

Regularly ask customers for testimonials to ensure you provide an accurate picture of your current success.

Also, keep your customers updated on your plans to create new solutions so they can invest in the future of your business.

Planning and writing the copy

The first points to address in this phase are Intent and Capabilities as you can write about these in the first person.

Look at the problem your product or service solves from your ideal customer's perspective and answer the following questions.

Provide as much honest, personal detail as you can to show you empathise with your prospect's pain.

Why are you offering your product or service?

Example niche: self help

Every time I had to do a presentation at work, I froze.

I knew my stuff, but something about speaking in front of a large group of people terrified me. It was incredibly frustrating.

I hated the awkward, hesitant version of myself that mumbled on stage.

That's why when I found some simple techniques that helped me get over my stage fright, I knew I had to share them.

What qualifications or skills do you have in the field?

Example niche: spiritualism

A week after my 21st birthday, I packed my bags and flew to Peru.

There I met Rosendo, an elderly guy who said he was a curandero, a healer who specialises in natural plant-based medicines.

He took me to a wooden temple in dense jungle just outside Iquitos, where he introduced me to ayahuasca and my healing began.

Testimonials

Now that you've established your credentials, source at least four, but up to 10, testimonials that address the questions below.

Does the solution work?

Example niche: weight loss

"I've always been a big guy and I hate depriving myself of food, so when my wife bought Carb Cycle for us to try together I was sceptical. I have to say though, the program is amazing. I've lost over 5 kilos in a month and I'm never hungry!"

How good is the service you provide?

Example niche: pets

"I accidentally ordered the wrong type of food for my cat. I called Pet Mart to let them know and they expressed me a new batch for no extra charge. Amazing service!"

What have you achieved in the past?

Example niche: making money online

"I signed up to Affiliate King over 12 months ago and in that time I've managed to grow my business to over $10,000 a month of passive income. I probably spend around 4 to 5 hours a week working on my site and the rest of my time is for me. Tony, I can't thank you enough, you've changed my life!"

What are you achieving now?

Example niche: investing

"I made a couple of the recommended trades in Kristy's weekly report and made a $1,564 profit. It was a good start, but I was worried it was just a lucky run. I increased the size of my trades and followed the suggestions in her next report and made $4,567! Kristy is the real deal."

PHASE 5 – CONVERT

Y ou've earned your prospect's trust by proving your solution works.

Now, you need to convince them to hit that buy button.

The **Convert Phase** is the second most important phase of the sales journey.

Even if your prospect skips the detail in the other phases, you can guarantee they have at least read your headline and, if they're interested, want to know how much your solution costs.

This phase is your chance to:
- set a price
- slash it, and
- sweeten the deal.

Content objective

Provide three time-limited offers that progressively increase the benefits to the prospect before providing an opportunity to purchase.

Emotional objective

Move the prospect from the excitement of a new offer to the fear of losing it three times before closing the sale.

Chemical objective

Trigger three spikes of dopamine that culminate in the highest peak with the purchase opportunity.

The value of urgency and scarcity

Convincing your prospect they need to act now to secure your offer is key to significantly increasing conversions from your marketing.

If the prospect knows they can return to your site whenever they want and purchase your solution for the same price, they're less likely to buy it right now.

Why would they? What's the rush?

You need to give the prospect a clear window of time for when the product or service can be purchased for the price you're offering.

You can do this by:

Simply stating in your conversion copy when the offer ends (I can only afford to offer this amazing introductory price for 1 more week! Don't miss out!)

Featuring a countdown clock that tells prospects exactly how long they have before the offer ends (Huge summer sale ends in 01 days : 02 hours : 03 mins : 41 secs)

Offering a special deal on a product that ends when the batch runs out, and showing how many items you currently have left in stock (Only $2.98 [5 left] 10 people currently viewing)

Cognitive biases to target

There are three powerful cognitive biases to target in this phase that impact how we value opportunities and respond to risk.

Loss aversion

How it works

The fear of losing something is typically more powerful than the desire to gain something.

We'd all love $1 million, but would you risk $500,000 on a 50/50 gamble to get it? (If you would you're either incredibly wealthy or have a serious gambling problem)

How to use it

Provide value for a limited time to motivate the prospect to take immediate action.

Zero-risk bias

How it works

We prefer options that totally eliminate a single risk over options that greatly reduce multiple risks without eliminating them, even when the later option is a superior choice.

How to use it

Remove as much risk as possible from the purchase process to ensure the prospect is comfortable buying from you.

Hyperbolic discounting

How it works

We prefer smaller immediate benefits to larger delayed benefits.

Most people would rather receive $10 today than $20 in a year, even though waiting a year delivers double the benefit.

How to use it

It's no secret that people love discounts. If a prospect is still not convinced to purchase, a genuine discount could be all the push they need to hit the buy button.

Planning the copy

Offer 1 – provide a benefit

Provide a bonus for a limited time to encourage greater investment in the offer and trigger loss aversion.

Creating your bonus

The best bonus deals enhance the original offer by providing a related benefit.

For example, if you were offering a guide on making money through blogging, your bonus could be:
- a podcast featuring interviews with successful bloggers,
- 10 bonus blog designs, or
- a discount on entry to an online course you provide on blogging.

It's best to plan your bonus early to provide a cohesive and compelling offer.

When planning your solution, highlight non-essential components or information you can later build into a bonus.

Create the solution and then separate out the non-essential elements when you're done.

If you're stretched for time or your solution is already complete, look for non-essential parts you can separate, or complementary components or information you can provide.

Offer 2 – remove or reverse risk from the purchase

Provide a free trail or money back guarantee for a limited time to trigger zero risk bias and make it as easy as possible for the prospect to justify the purchase.

You can even reverse the risk of making a purchase by offering to replace a product and refund the customer's money.

Free trials are particularly effective during the **Convert Phase**, as the longer the prospect trials your product or service, the greater the effect of the sunk cost fallacy.

Other ways to remove risk from the purchase process include:

Using a trusted payment processing provider to ensure the prospect feels safe giving you their payment details.

Offering your solution via a subscription model that allows customers to select the frequency and size of payments.

Offering buy now pay later options like Afterpay.

Offer 3 – establish the value of the bundled offer, then slash it

Create an estimate of what the different components of your bundled offer should cost and then slash that price with a discount.

Be generous but realistic when valuing the bundled offer.

You can value for offers for whatever you like, but if the prospect doesn't believe the value is genuine, they also won't be excited by a discount.

Provide the discount for a limited time to take advantage of the prospect's weakness for hyperbolic discounting and give them one final push to purchase.

It's important not to undervalue your offer during this phase as doing so could lead the prospect to question its quality.

Most people are happy to pay for quality, especially if there's a reasonable discount on top.

As a rule of thumb:
- **Up to 50% off discounts** – are enticing to prospects and won't damage their perception of the quality of your product or service. Most of your discounts should be in this range.
- **50%-80% off discounts** – are amazing deals that should

be saved for big promotions such as an introductory offer on a new product, otherwise you risk damaging the perception of your product or service by seeming desperate.

- **80%+ off discounts** – trigger the 'too good to be true' reflex and will lead the prospect to assume you either initially overpriced your solution or that it's of poor quality. Save these discounts for garage sales and police auctions.

Writing the copy

The second person perspective (you) is key to writing the **Convert Phase**.

It allows you to immerse your prospect in the offer and dial up the sense of urgency to drive the conversion.

When writing this phase, focus on conveying how exciting the offers are and how limited they are.

Offer 1

Launch week bonus: Low Impact Exercise Guide valued at $28!

To help you burn even more fat, I'm throwing in my low impact exercise guide as a bonus until the end of the week!

This easy-to-follow guide includes over 20 short, effective, low impact workouts you can do at home or when travelling using just your body weight.

You can create the sleek, fit body of your dreams in the comfort of your home or a hotel room without using any equipment.

This book normally retails for $28, but if you hurry you can pick up a copy as a bonus!

Offer 2

I'm so confident Carb Cycle will help you lose weight and keep it off, if you're not happy after 30 days, you can keep the program and I'll give you your money back!

I promise, if you follow Carb Cycle for just four weeks and don't lose weight, gain energy and start feeling better about yourself, I'll refund your money and you can keep the program to try again.

The only thing you have to lose is your extra weight.

Offer 3

Carb Cycle offers $164 of value!

The program includes the:
- *Diet Manual - valued at $58*
- *Shopping Guide - valued at $36*
- *Recipe Book - valued at $42, and*
- *Launch bonus: Low Impact Workout Manual - valued at $28.*

That's powerful, life-changing information valued at a total of $164.

To celebrate the launch of Carb Cycle, until Sunday 8 September, I'm offering the entire program:

Not for $164

Not for $123 (25% off)

Not even $82 (50% off)

But only $41! (75% off)

That's right, you can lose weight and transform your health and happiness with Carb Cycle for just $41!

But you have to hurry!

This amazing launch week offer must end in:

[03 days : 04 hours : 02 mins : 29 secs]

Complete Carb Cycle Program:

$41.00

Risyl Lejos

[Buy now] (button in bright colour)

CHEAT CODE CHEAT SHEET

This cheat sheet is your quick reference guide to setting up your sales page.

It's designed to help you check that you've met all the objectives for each phase of the COSS.

Attention

Objectives
- Content – Provide just enough information to encourage the prospect to read on
- Emotional – Generate surprise
- Chemical – Induce a spike of dopamine

Video
- Use your sales page as a script
- Provide captions for social media

Image
- Select an engaging, well-lit photo that communicates a single concept

Choose a headline strategy
- Make a bold claim
- Show undeniable proof
- Ask intriguing questions
- Tell an emotional story
- Highlight a strange fact or feature

Create a curiosity gap headline

- Provide some information
- Leave some information out your prospect will be desperate to know

Problem

Objectives
- Content – Frame the problem, then make it larger
- Emotional – Amplify frustration into anger
- Chemical – Cortisol replaces dopamine

Questions to answer
- What is the problem your ideal customer needs solved?
- How does the problem make your ideal customer feel?
- How have others tried and failed to solve the problem in the past?
- What are three statistics your prospect may not know about the problem?
- What are three facts your prospect may not know about the problem?

Solution

Objectives
- Content – Explain in detail how your solution solves the problem
- Emotional – Harness satisfaction to inspire hope
- Chemical – Trigger another dopamine spike

Questions to answer
- What are five important features of your solution?
- How will these features benefit your ideal customer?
- What are five benefits of solving the problem that your ideal customer could experience in the future?

Proof

Objectives
- Content - provide evidence your solution works and you understand your niche
- Emotional - Earn the prospect's trust

- Chemical - Oxytocin replaces dopamine

Display the '4 Cores of Credibility'
- Integrity
- Intent
- Capabilities
- Results

Questions to answer
- What compelled you to create your product or service?
- What qualifications or skills do you have in the field?

Testimonials to source
- Does the solution work?
- How good is the service you provide?
- What have you achieved in the past?
- What are you achieving now?

Convert

Objectives
- Content – Provide three time-limited offers
- Emotional – Move from excitement to fear
- Chemical – Trigger three dopamine spikes, saving the biggest for last

Create urgency and scarcity
- State when your offer ends
- Include a countdown clock
- Offer a deal that ends when the product runs out

Provide three offers
- Offer 1 – Provide a benefit
- Offer 2 – Remove or reverse risk from the purchase
- Offer 3 – Establish the value of the bundled offer, then slash it

JOIN ME ON FACEBOOK

Enjoy the book?

Want to find out more about how you can harness the power of the subconscious mind to supercharge your sales?

Join the Cheat Code Marketing group on Facebook.

Simply type **Cheat Code Marketing** into the search bar in Facebook and join.

Don't worry there aren't any annoying questions to answer.

This group is where I share all the latest content tips, tricks, insights and strategies to help you sell more in less time with far less effort.

A bit about me

I'm a career copywriter and content marketer obsessed with discovering what makes us tick.

With heaps of experience in creating high converting content for ad agencies, corporate marketing teams and my own business, I'm an expert in convincing people to hit that buy button.

When I'm not travelling around the world showing brands and businesses how to skyrocket their sales, you'll find me enjoying a pale ale or two in Sydney with Scooch, my 5-year old Bulldog, by my side.